UNLOCKED

Charleston, SC

www.PalmettoPublishing.com

Unlocked

First Edition

Paperback ISBN: 979-8-88590-515-2

eBook ISBN: 979-8-88590-516-9

UNLOCKED

3 KEYS TO OPEN YOUR FULL POTENTIAL

WILLIAM VAUGHN IV

TABLE OF CONTENTS

Intro   1

The Motivation Behind Unlocked

Chapter 1   5

Key #1 – Inspiration (The Inner Picture)

Chapter 2   23

Key #2 – Introspection (The Inner Labor)

Chapter 3   47

Key #3 – Implementation (The Outer Labor)

MINDSET SHIFT DECLARATIONS

(Say Words Below Out Loud Before You Read This Book)

- I expect radical, noticeable, and sustainable change to occur in my life as a result of reading and applying the principles of this book!

- I anticipate and openly welcome life-altering break-throughs to happen in my mind, my relationships, my money, and my overall well-being as a result of reading and applying the principles of this book

- I will no longer continue to settle for a life that is less than my full God-given potential

- I am now being transformed into the best version of who God has created me to be

INTRO
(The Motivation Behind "Unlocked")

YOU ARE GOING TO DIE ONE DAY! What a way to start off a book huh? Well it's the truth. We all are going to die one day. When you accept this as a fact of life and don't avoid that reality, then you are on your way to actually living a fulfilled life. If you know you are going to die one day and only have one life to live, why not live every day to your full potential? Why keep living a mediocre "barely making it" existence?

Let me ask you a question. Are you 100% satisfied with your life right now? If your answer is "YES" then you should close this book now and go on with your life. A person who is satisfied with their life doesn't have a strong motivation or desire to change how their life is going. The sad thing about being satisfied with our life is that most people have learned to adapt themselves to an unsatisfying and mediocre life to such a degree that they actually begin to *think* they are really satisfied and happy. However, deep down inside they have

www.pit2palace.org

suppressed their true dreams and desires for temporary comfort and security.

This book isn't meant for everyone. You probably are thinking "Well don't you want me to read your book?" Ironically, my goal is not for you to read this book but to heed this book. It is not the books you read that change your life. It is the books you *heed* that change your life. I'm not writing this just to say I wrote a book. I have experienced mind-blowing breakthroughs and transformation in my life as a result of what you are about to read and I want others to experience that in their lives. Are you still interested so far?

> The vast majority of people are merely "existing" but not really "living!"

So let me ask you again. Are you 100% satisfied with your life right now? If your answer is "NO" then it is a must for you to keep reading like your life depended on it *(because it actually does)!* To know you are not currently living up to your full potential in any area of your life and to keep doing the same things over and over again is equivalent to dying because your true God-given destiny is dead within you. I don't know about you, but my attitude is "What is the point of living if I'm going to live beneath my true purpose and potential?" The

vast majority of people are merely "existing" but not really "living!" I was once one of those people so I know. It's time for you to stop existing and to start living the life that God has created you for. We only have 1 life to live so why not live at our highest potential while we are living it?

The 3 keys of unlocking your full potential and destiny mentioned in this book are not just a cool topic or something to just write about. These are the 3 keys that personally empowered me to overcome tremendous obstacles and adversities in my own life. I have experienced numerous setbacks and seeming failures in my life. A few years ago through a series of bad business partnerships that produced failed deals and loss of revenue, I found myself face to face with more than a million dollars worth of obligations and debts to pay off with no visible way of being able to pay it at that moment. I was being swamped with phone calls, emails, text messages, and threats demanding payments that I did not have at that point in time. I'm talking about some serious pressure!!! I didn't even want to answer my phone most of the time because I knew it was probably another debt collector. People were doubting me, questioning me, and giving up on me all at the same time. I literally had to sell spare equipment and items I had

around the house that I wasn't currently using just to make ends meet for a temporary period.

I had heard about other business people getting in the hole by 6 or 7 figures, but I never in a million years would have imagined I would find myself in the same predicament. But there I was.... face to face with my own financial "Goliath." Even though I had a giant situation running towards me full speed, I have discovered that it is not the giants that come against us that destroy us. *It is the giants we refuse to face and conquer that destroy us!* No matter what giant we face in life, there always has been, always is, and always will be a "Giant Killer" bigger than any giant that opposes and threatens us. So the question is how to get the "Giant Killer" working on our behalf?

> It is the giants we refuse to face and conquer that destroy us!

Through the same 3 keys that will be outlined in this book in depth I was able to get "Unlocked" in my life and saw life-changing turn arounds and triumph over all opposition seeking to make me quit on my dreams and destiny. *I saw debts erased, destiny revealed, and dreams fulfilled by using these same 3 keys!* I was face to face with a situation that was at that moment far bigger than my ability to deal with

or overcome and this thought went through my head, "I only have 2 choices...choice #1 - Lay down, quit, and accept defeat. Or choice #2 - Rise up, face my giants, and bounce back better than ever with a story of triumph!" When those two options clearly appeared in the "fork in the road" in my mind, my winning nature inside would not let me quit and accept my current situation as my final outcome. I knew I would have to face my wife, my kids, my friends, my family and one day my Maker, so I refused to have an attitude or mindset that knew I had quit and accepted an outcome of mediocrity and failure. I am a firm believer that *"failing does not make someone a failure."* The only time we become a failure is when we fail to make adjustments and fail to keep going forward towards our goals and dreams.

> *Failing* does not make someone a *failure.*

As you read the following pages of this book, my heart's desire is that the content you absorb will produce breakthroughs in you and for you to set your life on the path of you being "Unlocked" in every area of your life! Buckle up for your ride to the next level!!!

CHAPTER 1

(Key #1 – "Inspiration" – The Inner Picture)

"A life without INSPIRATION is no life at all!"

The Real Meaning Of Inspiration

The 1st key you need to unlock your full potential and destiny individually, in your family, or in your organization/business is INSPIRATION. The word "Inspiration" has been watered down in today's society to a mere emotional feeling of wanting to do a certain task. Someone might say I feel "inspired" to go for a walk or I feel "inspired" to go on a vacation. There's nothing wrong with going on a walk or a vacation, but the real meaning and depth of the word "Inspiration" is so much bigger than just doing common life activities. Before we go

www.pit2palace.org

any further, to gain a better grasp of how deep Inspiration really goes let's look at its root definition.

The word "Inspiration" originates from the Latin word which first meant "to breathe into" and also had the meaning of "divine or supernatural guidance and influence on the mind" - (*webstersdictionary1828.com/Dictionary/inspiration*). So how does this definition of Inspiration apply to your life right now? There is a dream, a destiny, and a purpose that God Himself *"breathed into"* you from the day you were born. Throughout the course of your life you will experience *"divine and supernatural guidance and influence"* in many ways that are strategically designed to help you walk into what has already been *"breathed into"* you. These "divine and supernatural" leadings can come in many forms – *coincidentally* meeting the right person at the right time, seeing the very commercial of what you have been wanting to do, a phone conversation, a dream, reading a book (*wink wink*) and the list goes on. So now that you have a better understanding and more meaningful definition of Inspiration, it's time to start learning how to use this key to unlock your full potential.

> INSPIRATION is what has been "breathed into" you.

Is Your Inspiration Suffocating?

It's no coincidence the word Inspiration has the meaning of "to breathe into" and even medically has been used to refer to breathing oxygen into the lungs as well. What this means is that Inspiration is so vital to our life it is equated with the very act of breathing oxygen into our lungs. *To live a life without Inspiration is to die of suffocation!* Is your marriage suffocating? Is your dream and goal for your life suffo-cating? Inspiration is the oxygen to

> To live a life without Inspiration is to die of suffocation!

your dream and destiny! As you continue reading may new life and new oxygen be breathed into you to revive the suffo-cating dreams and destiny inside of you.

Now let's get brutally honest. Life is not peaches and cream and walks in the park everyday. There are many opposing forces and influences that come against us in life that seek to suffocate our potential and Inspiration. It could be nega-tive family interactions, a broken marriage, financial setbacks, loss of a loved one, the media, fear of failing, or even being overly concerned with other people's opinions of us. All these different situations can cause us to live beneath our potential

and to just "go with the flow" of life. But let me tell you this. You were not created to "go with the flow." You have been uniquely manufactured to "create your own flow" by operating in your full potential. But your full potential can only be unlocked if you are willing to awaken your inner Inspiration.

Sometimes when I drive to my company office in the mornings, I am always surprised to see people speeding in their cars, breaking traffic laws, and risking their lives and the lives of others just to be on time to a job they hate. Has this ever been you or is it still you? Yes you must take care of today's responsibilities and pay your bills by working, but don't stop pursuing your dream, your potential, and your Inspiration in the process. Pursuing and possessing your dream will eventually resolve your routine responsibilities. Go for the big thing and it will eventually take care of the little things. Don't neglect the big thing to only take care of little things. We all must take care of the little and unexciting things in life but when our Inspiration is alive and well inside of us then we always have something to look forward to even when we are doing tasks we don't really want to do. Even if you are working a job you hate and that doesn't excite you, when your potential is being unlocked and Inspiration is alive within

you, you will use every free second you have to think about and pursue that Inspiration until it becomes a tangible reality. Inspiration is your inner passion, and as you aggressively pursue your inner passion the steps to fully experience it will be revealed to you.

Staying Inspired When Circumstances Don't Appear Inspiring

There is a verse in the Bible that perfectly shows us how to stay inspired in the midst of contradicting facts. Hebrews 11 is widely regarded as the "Hall of Faith" making reference to numerous people throughout history who have had unique and unusual stories of living out their Inspiration to see uncommon results in their lives. In verse 27 of this same chapter, it makes reference to Moses when he fled from Egypt into the wilderness by saying "By faith he forsook Egypt, not fearing the wrath of the king; for he endured, as seeing *Him Who is invisible.*" I make reference to this verse not to talk about the life of Moses but to talk about your life and the secret to walking into what has already been "breathed into" you. The last part of this verse says "...for he endured, as seeing Him Who is invisible." This sounds like a contradicting statement

on the surface. My question is...."How can you see what is invisible?" The very definition of the word invisible means to not be seen.

Let me ask you a quick question. Have you ever "seen" a thought before? Do you see thoughts walking down the street or at the store? Of course

> Thoughts are invisible realities that when focused on consistently will eventually produce the visible equivalent.

not! We don't physically see thoughts, but thoughts are the way we can consistently "see" what is invisible to our physical eyes. *Thoughts are invisible realities that when focused on consistently will eventually produce the visible equivalent.* Inspiration will come in the form of thoughts and inner images that ignite your inner passion. Another word for this is IMAGINATION.

The Connection Between INSPIRATION & IMAGINATION

As seen above in the earlier section, Inspiration is like oxygen. But even in nature, oxygen must have two parts to make it what it is. It is referred to as O_2 which means two oxygen molecules put together make what we know as oxygen that

we breathe. IMAGINATION is without a doubt the second *oxygen* molecule needed to unlock our dream life and full potential. The word IMAGINATION is made up of two words – "Image" & "Nation". So an easy definition for Imagination is a "nation of images." Our Imagination is a nation of images in our mind. The nations of the world are classified as 1st World, 2nd World, and 3rd World based on the quality of life pro- vided for its citizens. Many immigrants flee away from 3rd world countries to find a better life or more opportunities in 1st world countries. In the same way, the quality of the nation of images you keep in your mind will determine if you live a 1st world life, 2nd world life, or 3rd world life no matter what country or region you physically live in. There are countless people who were born in 3rd world countries but who kept a 1st world Imagination consistently in their thoughts. Eventually because of the quality of Imagination they permitted to dwell in their minds their physical state matched their mental state opening up a new quality of life for them. On the opposite end of the spectrum, there are countless people who were phys- ically born in a 1st world country but they allowed 3rd world quality thoughts to reside permanently in their minds causing them to live a beggarly and defeated life even though they are

surrounded by limitless opportunities everyday. Inspiration and Imagination build the inward ladder to help you climb out of any undesired circumstance. It is impossible to maintain a top quality Imagination and remain in a bottom level lifestyle. It is equally impossible to maintain a bottom level Imagination and to rise to a top level lifestyle.

> It is impossible to maintain a top quality Imagination and remain in a bottom level lifestyle.

Genesis 11:6 (KJV) refers to a group of people trying to do a seemingly impossible task of building a tower to heaven. This scripture powerfully says, *"...now nothing will be restrained from them, which they have imagined to do."* Our ability to imagine is our ability to surmount every obstacle and to do what others say is impossible. If Inspiration is our "Inner Picture," then Imagination is the paintbrush that paints that picture within our minds. What you see on the inside is far greater than what you see on the outside. Your inner picture has the power to change your outer reality! If you don't like what you see in your life right now, then you need to immediately work on changing your inner picture to your ideal

life. Focusing consistently on your Inspired inner picture will eventually change your present outer reality to match your new inner picture.

In Genesis 13:15 (KJV) we see a perfect example of Inspiration and Imagination at work. God was speaking to Abraham leading him to take new territory and possess new promises and He spoke these powerful words, "For all the *land which you see*, to you will I give it. " Everything that Abraham could "see" he could "seize." This is a universal principle. A popular saying words it like this, "If you can conceive it, you can achieve it." That is a law of life just like the law of gravity. It will work every time it is implemented. No one ever had a great accomplishment or success without first "seeing" it within themselves. *If you don't first see it on the inside, you will never have it on the outside!* This is not just a one time "seeing" or a fantasy

> If you don't first see it on the inside, you will never see it on the outside.

you had when you were a little kid. You must have a fixed and permanent image in your mind that you guard and refuse to waver from to get your desired results.

Guarding Your Life From Inspiration Killers

When you want to plant a garden, you must plant your seeds and then protect the seed throughout the entire process until your full harvest comes in. You have to kill weeds, put out scarecrows, water the seed, and fertilize the seed in order to see what you planted come to its full potential. In the same way, your inner Inspiration & Imagination must be guarded and protected from the "weeds" of doubt, the "crows" of naysayers, and the "droughts" of delays. Failing in this process of protection is why most dreams or goals never happen. Most people get all excited about their dream or goal at first, but when opposition comes and "Inspiration Killers" show up they quit and retreat back to the known territory of comfort and perceived security. How you respond to opposition determines if you qualify for your inner Inspiration to go from theory to your actual reality. All of the great and successful people throughout history never allowed opposition or external circumstances to destroy their inner Inspiration and desired outcome. May you be in that same list of the greats in your life!

One of the greatest "Inspiration Killers" is the opinion of other people. Everyone has their own opinion about what you're doing or what you're not doing. But at the end of the day you can't live your life based on the opinions of other people at the expense of your own Inspired Life. I personally was guilty of this for a while in my own life of not pursuing my full potential and dreams because I cared about what other people may say or think about me in certain ways. One day as I was really reflecting on the current unfulfilled state of my life these words came into my mind. "*When you get so consumed with God's opinion of you, you will be free from man's opinion of you!*" This is in no way is intended to be a religious state-ment but an inner reality that can liberate you from being a slave to the opinions of other people. At the end of the day and when we take our last breath, the only opinion of us that matters is the opinion of the One Who created us. I remem-ber this like it was yesterday when those words came to me I literally felt like a boulder had been lifted off of my shoulders. I had been so concerned with other people's opinions in my life that I would suppress and minimize my own dreams and Inspiration so I wouldn't make other people feel a certain way

about me. These words gave me the confidence and ability to start stepping out into the true purpose and Inspiration that had always been inside of me but was covered up by fear and caring about what others might think. I say these words as loud and bold as possible..."FORGET WHAT THEY THINK!" When it comes to your dream, your goals, and your destiny the opinions of other people are irrelevant. This doesn't mean you can't take advice or counsel from someone else as we all need wise counsel to get the best results. However, you DO NOT need another person's permission or approval to pursue what is inside of your heart to do. If someone else doesn't approve of what you're doing, you can respectfully listen to their words and do it anyway. Most times when you act on your Inner Inspiration it will produce such phenomenal results in your life that the same ones who doubted and disapproved you will be congratulating you and want to know how they too can step out into their Inspired Life. Most times when people disapprove of your dream and your Inspiration, they are merely projecting their own fears and acceptance of an "un-inspired life" onto you. Basically if they aren't living their dreams, they don't think someone else can either. Even if you step out and fail, at least you had courage to step

out. *I would rather fail at pursuing my dream than to succeed at living a mediocre existence.* If you persist towards your Inspiration with aggressive tenacity and truthful willingness to make adjustments when needed, you will eventually arrive at your desired destination whatever that may be to you.

> I would rather fail at pursuing my dream than to succeed at living a mediocre existence.

Inspiration is not just about getting to a destination. It is about becoming a uniquely inspired person who is free to "be" and "do" what you are truly passionate about. You don't have to fit in other people's boxes anymore *(not even the ones you have created for yourself).* Don't share your Inspiration with everyone in its "infancy stage" because it may not be strong enough to endure naysayers and doubters. Just like a newborn child when they are an infant, they need a parent or guardian to feed and protect them until they get strong enough to survive on their own. When you have a "newborn" passion and Inspiration inside of you in any area of your life, you must at first feed it and protect it at all costs until it gains momentum and clarity to produce your desired result. Everyone will not support your dream or even understand it,

especially those closest to you. People have a tendency to want you to stay the same as you have always been because they themselves are staying the same that they have always been. You must surround yourself with others who are actively pursuing their Inspiration. The people you surround yourself with will add fuel to your "Inspiration Tank" or deplete your tank until your dream and passion runs out of gas and comes to a complete stop. Find other dreamers to fuel your dream! It is an old cliché but a true statement that "birds of a feather flock together." Eagles don't fly with pigeons! If you have an "eagle" Inspiration don't go around sharing it with "pigeon mentality" people. The pigeons will always tell you why it *can't* be done instead of why it *can* be done! Eagles still fly

> If you have an eagle Inspiration don't go around sharing it with "pigeon mentality" people!

high no matter what other birds do or don't do. May your Inspiration cause you to rise like the eagle you were created to be. Don't settle for a lesser life anymore! You only have one life to live so you might as well start living to your full potential.

Unlocking "INSPIRATION" Assignment

Really think about and write out your answers to the following questions to begin Unlocking your INSPIRATION:

What are 3-5 things about you that make you unique?

_____

_____

_____

_____

_____

If you could do anything you wanted everyday, what would it be?

_____

_____

_____

_____

_____

What is your perfect job, career, or hobby that you would love using your time talent and resources to do?

_____

_____

_____

_____

_____

If you could describe a marriage, family, and household that reflected real Inspiration how would you describe it?

_____

_____

_____

_____

_____

Special Assignment

(Creating An "Inspiration Dream Board")

An "Inspiration Dream Board" also known as a Vision Board is a powerful tool in helping you to intentionally keep images consistently in front of you that match the life you truly desire. Society and the news will keep showing you images of disaster, death, and destruction so if you don't intentionally combat these negative images how will you ever rise to the life you really want to live? Remember the word IMAGINATION is made up of two smaller words – "Image" & "Nation" which creates a nation of images in your mind.

I have personally seen the power of utilizing an Inspiration Dream Board in my own life. My wife and I created our own Inspiration Dream Board and put it up in our bedroom on the wall. Many times it looked like my present circumstances were a direct contradiction to my ideal life that I had on my Inspiration Dream Board. This is when I had to be intentional and focused to see my dream begin to become a reality. Having the Inspiration Dream Board in front was planting the seed so I had to protect it during times of opposing evidence and circumstances.

One thing that will put extra fire and acceleration to your Inspiration Dream Board is to speak words of tangible reality over it. On days it felt like, looked like, and seemed like my dream wasn't happening, I would look at my Inspiration Dream Board and say *"I am now living my dream life! There is no problem, no obstacle, and no circumstance that will keep my dream from becoming a reality!"* Just "seeing" your dream in front of you is a great step but then you must start "saying" your dream before it physically happens if you will ever see it become a reality. I am a living witness that this stuff works! Even me writing this very book is a result of one of the goals and dreams on my Inspiration Dream Board. My marriage and family relationships are growing stronger every day. My finances and business are multiplying in profit and opportunities. Trust me it works! It will work for you too, if you put in the work to do it.

To help you visualize exactly what an Inspiration Dream Board is here are a few examples:

(Personalize yours using your very own real life pictures.)

Steps To Creating Your Very Own Inspiration Dream Board:

(This Exercise Applies To You Personally, Your Family, or Your Company)

- Use the answers from above for the framework and direction of your images and pictures
- Use the internet to search for & print out images that match your life of Inspiration (you can also use magazines, newspapers, etc.)
    - **Example**: If one of your goals is to have a happy, fulfilling, and thriving marriage and family then find pictures that match that image
    - **Example**: If one of your dreams is to use your talent and skills in a certain industry or business, then find images and pictures that align with that dream
- Buy a medium to large size poster board
- Tape or glue the images and pictures you printed/cut out to your Inspiration Dream Board
- Place your Inspiration Dream Board in a place you will see it daily (Pro Tip: Take a picture of your Inspiration Dream Board on your phone and make it your screen saver on

your phone. Also you can email that image to yourself and print out to put smaller versions of it in your vehicle, work place, and other places you will constantly see it.)

- Every time you see it quickly say these words out loud or something similar in your own words– *"I am now living my dream life! I will not stop grinding, hustling, and believing until it becomes a reality!"*

(If you have completely read this chapter, honestly answered the questions, and completed your own Inspiration Dream Board, you are well on your way to living your life of Inspiration.)

CHAPTER 2

(Key #2 – "Introspection" – The Inner Labor)

"Refusing to face the truth of ourselves is refusing to be the best version of ourselves."

So What Exactly Is Introspection?

Now that your Inspiration has been awakened and energized it's time to remove the blockages and hindrances that prevent your Inspiration from flowing into every aspect of your life. I'm sure at some point in your life you have experienced a sink or bathtub that has clogged up causing water, mildew, and even mold to build up inside of it. When the pipeline is clogged up, you must find a way to get it unclogged and unstuck so the water can flow as it was designed to. One

of the most popular household products is Drano which is a liquid gel that breaks up blockages and clogs in pipelines. Your Inner Inspiration is like the water, and the process of Introspection is like the Drano. Inspiration cannot and will not flow from within you if you don't first remove the clogs and blockages through consistent Introspection.

The word Introspection is not exactly a popular word that you hear every day. But it is probably one of the most important words we all need to incorporate into our daily lives. Let's take a deeper look into its real meaning. This is where the "rubber hits the road" as the saying goes.

INTROSPECTION is made up of two primary root words – "intro" and "spect." The word "intro" means *within or inwardly* and also carries the meanings of the origin or beginning of a thing. The suffix "spect" means "to look or to see" *(www.etymonline.com/word/introspect)*. That's where we get many words such as "inspect" and "spectacular." So bringing these definitions of "intro" and "spect" together we arrive at a meaning of Introspection which is simply the process of l*ooking within*. Introspection is the act of intentionally looking within ourselves to evaluate,

> INTROSPECTION is the process of *looking within*.

analyze, and interact with our inner state of being. This includes looking within at our emotions, thoughts, ideas, and desires. Just as someone takes a magnifying glass to get a closer and clearer look at an object, Introspection is the magnifying glass we must use to get a closer and clearer look at our true inward condition.

In the world of real estate, before any house or building is occupied by a resident, it must first be inspected. The purpose of the inspection is to evaluate the quality and condition of the structure. The condition of the building determines what its present value is and what its potential value could be. In the same way, Introspection is the process of us *inspecting* our inner structures to see if we need any repairs or upgrades to reach our maximum value and potential. The most valuable piece of real estate we can invest in is the "real estate" between our two ears A.K.A our minds. Without conducting a thorough inspection on a building or structure, there will be costly repairs and issues that could have been addressed and resolved in a better manner if the inspection had been completed. If you don't commit to the process of consistently performing "inner inspections" through Introspection you too will experience costly errors, setbacks, and disappointments

in your personal life, relationships, and career. Introspection is not a nice or cool thing to do when you feel like it. It is MANDATORY for living your life to its full potential!

The majority of people in society are actually afraid of Introspection because it may cause them to face and uncover some painful or ugly things from their life. This is exactly why most people never live out their true Inspiration and dream life. If you refuse to habitually live a life of Introspection, you will never live a life of real Inspiration. There are rare occasions where people act on their Inspiration and temporarily see some levels of success, but without Introspection it is not sustainable because they do not have the inner capacity to remain there. Introspection is a vital necessity to not only reach our full potential but to stay in that state of being permanently. Introspection does not produce "get rich quick" schemes or "overnight miracles."

It unlocks the "inner riches" that make it inevitable for outer riches and desired outcomes to be attracted to us.

> Until you are free to be the "true you" you will never experience the full potential that life has to offer you.

The purpose of Introspection is for the identification and removal of barriers and blockages that keep us from being

the most authentic and valuable version of ourselves. Until you are free to be the "true you" you will never experience the full potential that life has to offer you. As mentioned earlier in the book, I speak from absolute experience on this. I was a slave to the opinions and expectations of others in many areas of my life which would cause me to not pursue my own desires and Inspiration because I was overly concerned with what others would think about me. This is no way to live your life! It wasn't until I began doing deep and real Introspection in my own life that I saw the truth of areas of fear within me that I had to address. Once I applied the Drano of Introspection to my "inner pipelines" I literally saw my life rapidly and significantly change in my marriage, my finances, and my overall purpose right before my very eyes.

Applying Introspection To Unclog Your Inspiration "Pipelines"

If you buy a bottle of Drano at the store, it is of no real value until you actually open it up and use it. In the same way, simply reading this book or understanding the definition of Introspection isn't going to change or impact your life. *Acquisition of knowledge* is a waste of time without the

application of knowledge! It's not what you know that will unlock your full potential. It's only what you *KNOW* and *DO* that will release you to your next level! There are countless unsuccessful and unfulfilled people in the world who have tons of knowledge but for one reason or another they aren't applying it to see actual results in their life. This is because there is something clogging up their Inspiration "pipeline."

The Blockages Of Introspection

Introspection can only work if you are willing to truthfully look within yourself and not make excuses or justifications for what you may find. Introspection is like when you clean out underneath your couch cushions. There will usually always be junk you didn't know was there. However, there will be valuable items hidden there as well such as money, jewelry, and possessions you value that may have fallen out of your pocket somehow over time and got stuck under the cushions. Introspection will without a doubt shine light on the junk within us, but if we commit to the process it will also always unveil the treasures and valuable potential within us at the same time. There are literally "treasures" of potential within

you. Just like physical treasures you have to dig through the dirt first to get to the good stuff.

If Introspection is so valuable, then why don't more people do it? Many people have created defense mechanisms in their mind that oppose their ability to live out a life of true Introspection which in turn causes them to live a life beneath their full potential.

Let's take a deeper look at some of the main enemies and blockages of Introspection:

- Blaming Others
- Making Excuses
- Pride & Self-overestimation
- Busyness of life

Blaming Others

The "blame game" is a game you will always lose! Do you presently have disappointing circumstances in your life that you are blaming others for? Blaming others keeps countless people in a cycle of defeat and diminished results in their lives. Blame is the exact opposite of Introspection as it causes you to look "around you" for the

> The "blame game" is a game you will always lose!

reason why things aren't working instead of looking "within you" to find the real answer. The real answer is always within!

Let me be transparent for a moment. Some years ago in my own business endeavors I had some dishonest people to steal a large sum of money from my company. Of course, like anyone, my first thought was this was all their fault for why this happened. However, as I began my own process of Introspection and maturity as an individual and entrepreneur, I began to look *within* and see patterns of dysfunction in some of my business relationships. The more honest and open I looked at myself and my own inadequacies, I then began to see that it wasn't their fault for stealing the money *(even though they were morally and legally wrong)*. It was my own poor decision-making, lack of boundaries to have healthy business relationships, and lack of due diligence that even allowed it to happen. So when I shifted the blame from being "their" fault to being "my" fault that's when I began to make huge progress and to exponentially grow to the next level in my business and life of Inspiration. I had to admit that I wasn't making wise relationship and partnership decisions and that I wasn't being thorough enough in my due diligence processes. When I acknowledged and admitted the truth of

my own failures in the situation, the truth made me free from that cycle of dysfunction and "holes in my bucket" financially and began unclogging the "pipeline" for my life of Inspiration to flow like never before.

There are times when certain things that happen to us are 100% out of our control and others are to blame for their actions. However, in this case forgiveness is one of the ingredients of real Introspection. Forgiveness is simply the deliberate act of verbally, mentally, and emotionally releasing resentment, anger, and negativity directed towards another person. Are you willing to forgive that person who abused you, lied to you, or mistreated you? It isn't always easy to forgive others who have done us wrong, but it is necessary if you want to live your life to your full potential. Unforgiveness will always make you blame the person you *think* did you wrong or who actually did do you wrong. I use the word "think" because sometimes it is our own perception of a person or situation that makes us *think* we were done wrong versus them actually doing us wrong. Forgiveness is not so much for the other person as it is for our own inner

> Forgiveness is not so much for the other person as it is for our own inner well-being.

well-being. A famous quote by Marianne Williamson powerfully says "unforgiveness is like drinking poison and expecting the other person to die." If you are holding unforgiveness or resentment towards others, you are only poisoning your own life and future.

I believe the easiest way to forgive others is by first realizing our own imperfections and the fact that we at times will need others to forgive us. When I know that I am in need of forgiveness from others, then I can more easily forgive others. Even if someone is 100% to blame for an

> Our attitude is always in our control!

action against you, you can't control what they did or didn't do. However, you CAN control how you choose to respond! The actions of others are not in our control. *But our attitude is always in our control!* If you are tired of living a life beneath your full potential, make the decision now to stop blaming others and to start looking in the mirror at yourself of how you can grow and be better. When you do commit to this process of real Introspection, there is nothing that can stop you from rising to new heights and uncharted territories of success in whatever you do. There are only 2 options when someone has done us wrong – *become bitter or become better.* Refusing to

blame others and openly accepting the life of Introspection is the guaranteed way to overcome bitterness and to arise as the best version of yourself in every area of your life.

Say these words out loud to break free from blaming others and repeat as needed in the Introspection process.

"I will no longer blame others for the negative outcomes of my life. I cannot control what others do or don't do but I always do control my attitude and my response. I will ask forgiveness of those whom I have done wrong. I will extend forgiveness to those who have done me wrong. I refuse to be a slave of blame anymore. I willingly look in the mirror of myself and I take responsibility for the outcome and quality of my life whether it's good or bad. From this day forward I refuse to be bitter and I choose to be BETTER every day in all areas of my life!"

Making Excuses

Making excuses is similar to blaming others but its focus is slightly different. Blaming others focuses on projecting undesirable outcomes on people. Making excuses focuses on projecting undesirable outcomes on external circumstances. We just learned about forgiveness so forgive me if I step on

your toes a little. Here are some examples of excuses people make:

- "The reason I can't get a promotion is because they don't let people like me get higher positions."
- "I would open up that business, but I just don't have the money to do it."
- "I would go back to school to get certified, but you know I'm getting older and got kids now."
- "Our company can't grow because of the economy."
- "I can't get a good job because of my criminal background."
- "No one from my neighborhood or family has ever done that before."
- "My family would be better if my spouse and kids would just see things from my point of view."
- AND THE LIST GOES ON & ON...........

I understand that several of these things may be actual barriers that you or people you know have encountered in their life. However, *barriers are not immovable!* Let me say it again. *BARRIERS ARE NOT IMMOVABLE!* No matter what barrier you are facing whether it's a financial

> BARRIERS ARE
> NOT IMMOVABLE!

barrier, a family barrier, or a health barrier, when you commit to a life of INTROSPECTION you will always find the answer to overcome any barrier. So that means there is no reason and no excuse for you not to live the life of your dreams. There are only 3 reasons why you aren't moving forward in your life, your family, or your business. $_1Y._2O._3U!$ Until you honestly accept this, your life will not change for the better.

We must accept the fact that the real reason we aren't moving forward is because of something we are doing that we should stop doing or because of something we are not doing that we should start doing. It's really that simple. When I was face to face with extremely threatening obstacles in different areas of my life, I had to look in the mirror at my own self and honestly ask "Why is this happening and what do I need to change to get a different result?" The key word in that question is "I." It wasn't other people who needed to change. It wasn't the government that needed to change. It wasn't circumstances that needed to change. It was "I" that needed to change! When we focus our efforts and energy on changing "I" then that's

> It is always "I" that needs to change not others who need to change.

when the other areas of our lives will change because "I" is the common denominator in everything we do.

Excuses are like a prison that has locked up your full potential. If you are willing to break free from the prison of excuses, then and *only then* will you begin to experience life on a higher level of fulfillment. Here are some real life INTROSPECTION questions that you can ask yourself not just now but as a habitual lifestyle of inner examination to get the best results consistently. I will actually use the same list of excuses from above in this below section to show you how INTROSPECTION can produce breakthroughs instead of allowing an "excuse mentality" to produce bondage and mediocrity.

- **Excuse: *"The reason I can't get a promotion is because they don't let people like me get higher positions."***

    - Introspection Questions: What skills do I need to work on or acquire to be the top option for a promotion? How can I make myself a better asset to my boss and company? If I acquire the skills needed and there is no realistic option of promotion at my current company, what other companies are looking for higher level positions to be filled? How can I start my own company with these skills?

- **Excuse: *"I would open up that business, but I just don't have the money to do it."***
  - Introspection Questions: How can I save money from my current income to do it? Who can I partner with that has the money that would help me do it? What other side hustle or opportunity can help me make the extra money needed to do it?
- **Excuse: *"I would go back to school to get certified, but you know I'm getting older and got kids now."***
  - Introspection Questions: How can I get a babysitter for a couple hours each week so I can take my classes? How much earlier do I need to get up in the mornings to take classes before everyone else gets up? How can I stay up a little later in the evenings after everyone is sleep to finish the program? Is there a better job or position I can get that would pay for my school or give me flexibility to attend during the day?
- **Excuse: *"Our company can't grow because of the economy."***
  - Introspection Questions: What adjustments do we need to make in the current economic environment to stay profitable and progressive? Is the industry we

are in feasible to move forward or should we look at breaking into new sectors and industries that are thriving in this time? Who can we hire with the right skill set to help us profitably navigate these obstacles and challenges? How can we reduce expenses and increase revenue in a sustainable way?

- **Excuse:** *"I can't get a good job because of my criminal background."*

  ○ Introspection Questions: What companies are hiring not based on criminal backgrounds? How can I start my own business or company? What certifications and skills can I acquire to make me the most qualified person to get the position I want despite my past record?

- **Excuse:** *"No one from my neighborhood or family has ever done that before."*

  ○ Introspection Questions: How can I get around people who are doing what I want to do? If no one else I know has done this before, then how can I be the first one to do it? If I commit to doing everything needed to succeed in this industry, then why can't I do it?

- **Excuse:** *"My family would be better if my spouse and kids would just see things from my point of view."*

- Introspection Questions: In what ways can I seek to see things from their points of view? How can I be a better listener to their needs and desires? Are there any strong marriages and families I can connect with to learn from them to be a better spouse and parent?

As seen above Introspective questions are always geared towards solutions and possibilities. When you are "solution minded" and "possibility minded" you are literally unlimited in what you can do or accomplish in your life. The majority of people in the world are

> Be "possibility minded" instead of "problem minded."

"problem minded." Deciding to make the shift to being "possibility minded" in a "problem minded" world will give you an instant advantage in life to begin experiencing your life of real Inspiration. Don't allow excuses to keep you back from your potential and dream anymore!

Pride & Self-Overestimation

In order to live life at our highest potential, we can't have ego problems. Covid-19 was globally broadcasted as a world-changing pandemic, but pride and false self-images

are a far bigger pandemic than any virus. Pride is refusing to be honest about you really are. Social media has multiplied people's ability to project an image of themselves they want others to "think" that they are instead of being who they really are. Pride is when we over-estimate our own ability and under-estimate our need for the abilities of others to help us reach our full potential in life.

One of the greatest lies in the media is the concept of being a "self-made success." That is the essence of pride in its purest form. There is no such thing as a "self-made success." Everyone who has experienced any level of success has had to have other people in some capacity to give them tools, assistance, or opportunities to achieve that success. The sooner we can take our eyes off of ourselves, the sooner we can rise to the highest levels we were designed to occupy.

A prideful attitude is one of the primary reasons so many people don't experience fulfillment or real progress in their life. The prideful parent thinks they have all the answers and have nothing to learn from their children so they don't value their children's words or ideas.

> Don't allow pride to block your true value anymore.

This sends the children looking to other places to be heard

and valued *(even wrong places)*. The prideful boss or leader thinks they are the "top of the ladder" so no one else can tell them what to do or share ways of improvement for the organization causing stagnation, tension, and employee turnover. The prideful spouse thinks their way is the only way of doing things in the relationship so they don't listen to the needs of their significant other causing their relationship to suffer and grow stale. Pride is dangerous as it prevents us from receiving value from others because we think we are the most valuable or at least want to *appear* as the most valuable in our circles of life. Many times it is the value that others are designed to give us that will actually unlock and uncover the value that is within us. Don't allow pride to block your true value anymore!

An important aspect of Introspection is honestly asking ourselves, "Who can help me in the areas of my weakness to get to the results I want to see?" How can you apply this question to your family life, your financial life, or your organization? A prideful mentality will not allow you to ask this question because you want to be the center of your own decisions and think you don't need anyone else to help you. Some people falsely think that pride makes them appear strong when in actuality it is a weakness because you will be

lacking in areas that others are supposed to help you grow in. When you are free from your own pride, you can acknowledge your faults, weaknesses, and areas of ignorance which will position you to receive the answers and help you need in these areas. Humility is a necessary ingredient to reach our highest heights in life. As a parent, as a business owner, as a spouse, and in any area of life, it's only when we are willing to humble ourselves and to acknowledge our need for the help and perspective of others that we remove the ceiling of limitations from our growth.

You can never go higher when you have pride, because in your mind you think you are already at the peak of your performance. Humility is the understanding that there is no peak and there are always new levels to rise to that we can't arrive at on our own

> Humility is a necessary ingredient to reach our highest heights in life.

ability alone. This applies to your family, your company, and your dream! Embrace humility for "God opposes the proud, but He gives grace to the humble (*James 4:6 NKJV*)." Pride actually causes divine forces to work against you to prevent your breakthrough into the results you want to see. Humility attracts divine assistance to us from visible and invisible

sources to help us accomplish what we were designed and created to do.

Having a humble mindset allows you to honestly accept the not so pretty things that will appear in your process of Introspection. Humility activates ACCEPTANCE, ACKNOWLEDGMENT, and ADJUSTMENT! When we embrace a genuinely humble mindset, we can easily *Accept* our shortcomings and failures, *Acknowledge* our need for the help of others,

> Humility activates ACCEPTANCE, ACKNOWLEDGMENT, and ADJUSTMENT.

and *Adjust* accordingly to make the necessary changes for improved results. If you are tired of the way things have been going in any area of your life, then it is time to embrace humility which will initiate the transformation you are looking for in your life.

Say these words out loud to embrace humility in your life:

"I will no longer allow pride to hold me back from my highest potential. I acknowledge that I can't get the full results I want to see in my life without others helping me along the way. I embrace humility and openly welcome God's grace to catapult me to my next level of life! I will make the necessary adjustments in my thoughts, my interactions with others, my

www.pit2palace.org

attitude, and my decision making to be the best version of myself and the best asset to others!"

Busyness of Life

This area may sting a little bit. Just like a vaccine it may hurt initially but its outcome is designed to be to your benefit. We live in a society that thrives on entertainment whether its Youtube, Netflix, sports, or recreational activities. There is absolutely nothing wrong with our preferred method of fun and entertainment as we all want to have a good time and enjoy ourselves in certain ways. However, if your life is presently operating beneath your full potential, *entertainment* must take a backseat to *enlightenment.* This is where the word SACRIFICE comes in to play. If you want to live your dream, then you MUST be will-

> Don't mistake *busyness* for *progress!*

ing to sacrifice unfruitful and unprofitable activities that will not contribute to your dream becoming a reality. If you like hanging out with your friends on the weekend but they aren't contributing to your success or desired life, you have a choice to make. Keep hanging out with your unfruitful relationships, or live the life of your dreams? Some people may think "Well,

can't I do both?" If what you are currently doing is not producing the life you truly want to live, then you must make different decisions to see a different result.

Being overly busy can cause us to carry weights and baggage that will slow down or altogether stop our progress to our life of Inspiration and fulfillment. A commercial airplane cannot be legally authorized to take off the runway and soar to its destination if it has too much weight on board. Every passenger, the fuel, the luggage, and any other equipment all contributes to the carrying weight of the plane. If the plane takes off with too much weight, it will burn fuel too quickly to reach its intended destination. In the same way, you can't ascend to your fullest potential as a person, a parent, or financially until you remove unnecessary weight and baggage from your life.

Hebrews 12: 2 instructs us to "...*lay aside every weight*..." This is why being too busy is an enemy of Introspection. Instead of investing focused, purposeful time and thought energy on identifying and removing unnecessary weights, most people stay in their same cycle of an overly busy life and never deal with the real issues to produce lasting change. Every year countless people make New Year's resolutions to lose weight

in the upcoming year. This usually always refers to physical weight. Losing physical weight is a commendable goal, but the most valuable weights to lose are the internal weights, relationship weights, and time weights that are keeping you back from your life of Inspiration.

Do you keep experiencing failure after failure and then wonder why it's not working in some area of your life? Introspection requires times of *silence* and *separation*. It is in the quiet moments that we can clearly hear the "still small voice" of truth and change within us. Imagine this scenario for a moment. All of your TV's at your house are turned up to maximum volume. Your stereo system is blasting as loud as possible playing your favorite songs.

> It is in the quiet moments that we can clearly hear the "still small voice" of truth and change within us.

Your children are screaming at the top of their lungs running through the house. While all this is going on, your cell phone is sitting on the kitchen table ringing with the "opportunity of a lifetime" calling you. This is the call you have been hoping and waiting for but you couldn't hear it or answer it in time because of the chaotic and loud environment around you. You see the missed call an hour later and call back but

by then someone else has been offered the same opportunity and took the position.

Now you may be thinking that seems a little exaggerated but it's actually very accurate. Your internal mental environment can be so chaotic and loud to where you can't clearly hear the answers and directions to produce your desired outcomes in your life. We live in a fast paced society with all of the technology and activities available at our fingertips. We must be careful to not allow the busyness around us to drown out the voice of Introspection within us. Valuing silence in a world of chaos takes an intentional focus and decision. Don't mistake busyness for progress! A person running full speed on a treadmill is busy but when it is all said and done they will still be standing in the same exact place just out of breath, sweating, and tired. Introspection breaks us free from the "treadmill" of busyness and puts us on the path of unlimited progress.

Say these words out loud to prioritize Introspection in your life:

"I choose to embrace moments of silence and separation in my life to focus on what really matters without being distracted by the busyness around me. I will re-evaluate my

priorities of how I use my time, my energy, and my resources. I am willing to make the needed attitude adjustments, rela-tionship adjustments, and time usage adjustments to see true and lasting change in my life. Whatever sacrifices are required no matter how uncomfortable or inconvenient they may be I will make those sacrifices to begin living my life at my fullest potential. I desire change and transformation more than I desire comfort and convenience. I embrace the life of Introspection!"

Introspection Assignment

If you have completely read and participated in this section on Introspection you are well on your way to experiencing ongoing breakthrough and transformation in your life, your family, and your career/business. Introspection is asking yourself unbiased and objective questions with a willingness to accept the truthful answer no matter how uncomfortable or painful it may be.

Below is a list of up, close, and personal Introspection questions to start doing some "digging" to get to the trea-sures within you:

(Ask these questions out loud to yourself in a quiet place and listen inwardly to your thoughts for the answers that come to your mind.)

Why is my life not moving forward like I want it to?

_____

_____

_____

_____

_____

How come my personal and/or business finances are stuck and struggling?

_____

_____

_____

_____

_____

What relationships do I currently need to separate from that I know are draining my Inspiration energy?

_____

_____

_____

_____

_____

What is holding me back from separating from them even though I know the relationship is toxic or unfruitful?

_____

_____

_____

_____

_____

What are new relationships and environments I can connect with that will help me advance in my life of Inspiration in my areas of desired change?

_____

_____

_____

_____

_____

Who am I currently blaming for the present disappointments of my life and how can I shift the focus being "their" fault to taking personal ownership of my life?

_____

_____

_____

_____

_____

www.pit2palace.org

Who in my life do I need to forgive and to ask forgiveness of?

_____

_____

_____

_____

_____

Why do I keep working this same job year after year even though I hate it and know I should be doing something different?

_____

_____

_____

_____

_____

In what ways can I improve my communication skills and attitude towards my (spouse, kids, boss, employees, etc)?

_____

_____

_____

_____

_____

How can I embrace a life of Introspection and how will my life improve by doing so?

_____

_____

_____

_____

_____

If you are still hanging around after this chapter on the 2nd Key of Introspection, then you are pretty serious about changing. The above questions are to create momentum in making Introspection a way of life not just answering the questions in this book. There are literally unlimited questions we can ask ourselves to get to the root of issues and see breakthroughs and transformation. May new doors and new opportunities be opened to you as you have taken this journey so far!

> If you don't like the results in your life what are you going to DO about it?

CHAPTER 3

(Key #3 – "Implementation" – The Outer Labor)

"An ounce of doing things is worth a pound of theorizing."- Wallace D. Wattles

The Key That Physically Unlocks Your Potential

If you have ever used a combination lock before, you know it has multiple numbers that must align to be unlocked. The "secret digits" could be 1,2,3. If you only enter in the numbers 1 & 2, the possibilities behind the door still remain out of reach because the 3rd digit is missing. We have studied and looked deeper at key #1 and key #2 which are INSPIRATION and INTROSPECTION. However, it is the 3rd

key of IMPLEMENTATION that will release your dream, your purpose, and your inspired life into *Unlocked* status.

What Exactly Is Implementation?

The definition of Implementation is simple and easy. Implementation is simply *taking action on something*. It is the process of applying the necessary practical steps to cause an idea, a goal, or a strategy to become a tangible reality. I believe Implementation can be summed up in the profound yet simple slogan of Nike. Just do it! The world is full of talkers and dreamers but only few people actually DO what they are talking and dreaming about. That's why so few people actually live out their

> IMPLEMENTATION is simply *taking action on something*.

dreams. Having a dream or great idea without taking action is like having a brand new car but never putting gas in it. It can look good sitting in the "garage" of your mind, but without the "gasoline" of Implementation it will never go anywhere. There is a powerful and popular passage of scripture in the Bible that perfectly defines Implementation.

James 1:22-26 (NIV), *"Do not merely listen to the word, and so deceive yourselves. Do what it says. Anyone who listens to*

the word but does not do what it says is like someone who looks at his face in a mirror and, after looking at himself, goes away and immediately forgets what he looks like. But whoever looks intently into the perfect law that gives freedom, and continues in it - not forgetting what they have heard, but doing it - they will be blessed in what they do."

In just these few short verses, DOING a.k.a Implementation is mentioned 5 times. There must be an important point being made here. The *acquisition of knowledge* is useless without the *application of knowledge!* Please listen closely to what I'm about to say. The first sentence of these verses is telling us that if we acquire knowledge or information but don't actually Implement it or do it we are literally deceiving ourselves. That is a powerful statement to make. I am always shocked when struggling and unhappy people are presented with valuable knowledge that could drastically improve their life but they answer with these words, "I already knew that." My first and only thought when I hear unhappy people say this is, "Then why aren't you DOING it?" Refusing to do what you know or refusing to seek to know what you need to know will always keep you in a defeated and disappointed state of being.

Now let me get a little blunt on this part. The biblical reference we just saw in James 1:22-26 compares knowing without doing to looking at a physical mirror and then walking away and forgetting what you just looked at. What does that mean to us? The purpose of looking into a mirror is to check the status of our physical appearance and make any needed adjustments or improvements. When we wake up in the morning we all have physical appearance adjustments we must make – washing the crust out of our eyes from sleeping, brushing our teeth, fixing our hair, taking a shower, putting on deodorant, getting dressed, etc. (well at least I hope you do these things - LOL). Imagine if you wake up in the morning, look in the mirror, and then walk off and don't make the physical appearance adjustments you need to make. Where I'm from in the South we call that "trifling." That means someone does not care how they look or carry themselves. This is exactly what the verse above is saying for your life. If you gain knowledge that can transform the undesired results of your life but don't Implement that knowledge your life will be "trifling." If you don't like the results in your marriage or family right now what are you going to DO about it? If you don't like the results in your finances right now what are you going

to DO about it? If you know you are living beneath your full potential what are you going to do about it?

I have shared a few times in this book of my own past undesirable circumstances in my life. I had to make up my mind that I was going to rise up and DO whatever it took to get better results. I don't believe in crying or complaining about my problems. Crying and complaining won't change what you're crying and complaining about. *Only Implementing right knowledge will produce your desired outcomes in life.* Notice I said "right" knowledge. All knowledge is not equal. Growing up I would sometimes watch the famous trivia game show Jeopardy. Many people refer to the questions

> Only IMPLEMENTING "right" knowledge will produce your desired outcomes in life.

on Jeopardy as "useless information." The game show host would ask questions about all types of random topics and world events the majority of which are an interesting (or not so interesting) fact. The contestants would have to know these facts to win the game but the type of knowledge being displayed was not knowledge that would transform someone's deepest desires into a reality. Focus on the pursuit of "relevant" knowledge! Relevant knowledge is knowledge that

specifically applies to your tailor made Inspiration. That's why having your Inspiration unlocked is so vital.

How many people do you know that go to college for 2 years, 4 years, or even longer and then graduate and do absolutely nothing with the degree of knowledge they just acquired? They were acquiring knowledge but it may not have been "relevant" knowledge to the true potential inside of them. If someone wants to be a doctor, then what sense would it make taking classes to be a chef? If someone wanted to be an actress, then why would they be taking classes to be an office worker? If you say you want your life to change, your family to change, your money to change, or your organization to change I only have one question for you, "What relevant knowledge are you actively *pursuing* and consistently *applying* to produce the change you want to see?" Too many people are like ostriches and stick their head in the sand when confronted with undesirable circumstances instead of facing it head on, getting the necessary knowledge, and Implementing that knowledge to see a lasting change. It is now your time for Implementation to experience your life of Inspiration!

The Top 3 Enemies Of Implementation

No one in history ever did anything notable or great without having to overcome obstacles along the way. Don't think when you set out on the path of Implementation to move towards your goal or dream that it will be smooth sailing and sunny skies every day on the journey. *Obstacles are inevitable. But failure is optional!* You choose if you will be a failure by your decision to quit or keep going when you inevitably face these obstacles. There are many opposing forces that will seek to get you to lie down and quit on your dream. We will focus on 3 primary enemies that all of us will have to face on our journey to actually living out our life of Inspiration.

Implementation Enemy #1 - Fear of Failure

"What if I step out to do it and it doesn't work?" That is a real question and thought that comes to all of our minds when doing something new and making steps towards our true desires. The non-sugar coated truth is that there is a real possibility when you take action towards your goal it might not work out as you planned. Rarely does anything work perfectly the very first time. Every great inventor and innovator

would tell you this as well. In order to experience life at your full potential, it is MANDATORY that you change your definition and perspective of failure.

I mentioned in the introduction of this book that *"failing does not make anyone a failure."* It's only when we fail to make adjustments and fail to keep moving

> *Failing* does not make you a *failure!*

forward towards our goal that we become a failure. To help you reshape, redefine, and rethink your attitude towards failure here are some powerful quotes on this very topic.

- "Failure is not the opposite of success. It is part of success." – Arianna Huffington
- "I never lose. I either win or learn." – Nelson Mandela
- "Giving up is the only sure way to fail." – Gena Showalter
- "Failure should be our teacher, not our undertaker. Failure is delay, not defeat. It is a temporary detour, not a dead end. Failure is something we can avoid only by saying nothing, doing nothing, and being nothing." – Denis Waitley
- "I have not failed. I've just found 10,000 ways that won't work." – Thomas Edison
- "Success is stumbling from failure to failure with no loss of enthusiasm." – Winston Churchill

- "Every adversity, every failure, every heartache carries with it the seed of an equal or greater benefit." – Napoleon Hill
- "Do not judge me by my successes. Judge me by how many times I fell down and got back up again." – Nelson Mandela

I hope you are getting the point now. Stop being afraid to fail! All the greats have failed. All the legends have failed. It's how you respond to failure that will determine how much you succeed. The public school system grades us based on pass or fail and frowns upon failure which creates a mindset in us that failure is bad. The opposite is actually true. Failure is a mandatory part of discovering what works and what doesn't work to fine tune our journey to our life of Inspiration. A thought I constantly live by is "I would rather fail aiming for my dream than to succeed living a mediocre existence."

Implementation Enemy #2 - Waiting For Perfect Circumstances

When it comes to pursuing Inspiration, far too many people say "I will do it when *THIS* or *THAT* happens." Well what if *THIS* or *THAT* never happens? Don't make your dream or desired outcome in life contingent on something else happening first.

Do it anyway! Do it afraid! Do it NOW! Don't wait for the perfect time to take action pursuing your Inspiration. The "perfect" time will never come. There will always be obstacles, nuisances, and unfavorable situations happening around us. We just can't let these things stop us from our Implementation of the steps needed to see real change in our life.

I came across this powerful quote that perfectly applies to not waiting for perfect circumstances to take action on experiencing our life of Inspiration. "Life isn't about waiting for the storm to pass. It's about learning how to dance in the rain. – Vivian Greene" Taking action in the midst of adversity is a primary trait of those who live out their dreams. Stop sitting by waiting for the "right time" to pursue your potential. The time is always right to pursue your Inspiration. The time is NOW!

Implementation Enemy #3 - "Trying" vs. "Doing"

There are far more *dreamers* than doers in the world. Of course there is nothing wrong with being a dreamer. All great things started with a dream first. However, being a dreamer only and not being a doer is the reason most dreams never become a reality. Some people might say, "Well, I did try to

act on my dream and it still didn't work." *Trying* and *doing* are not the same! *Trying is only attempting something and quitting if it doesn't work. Doing is attempting something and not quitting until it does work.* Doing is taking consistent action, making necessary adjustments where needed, and refusing to quit until

> Stop being a "tryer" and start being a "doer!"

the desired outcome is reached. Don't be a statistic of those who "try." In the famous words of Yoda from Star Wars, "Do! Try not. Do. Or do not. There is no try." Stop being a "tryer" and start being a "doer" to unlock your life of Inspiration!

Using The 3 Keys To Unlock Your Full Potential

The 3 keys in this book MUST be used together to unlock the life you want to see. Let's quickly review each key:

- **Key #1 – Inspiration**
  - The potential that has been *breathed into* you
  - Your "inner picture" to create your outer reality
- **Key #2 – Introspection**
  - The process of *looking within* to examine your thoughts, habits, motives, and feelings

- ○ Your "inner labor" to remove blockages and barriers that prevent your Inspiration from becoming a reality
- **Key #3 – Implementation**
- ○ The process of *doing* what you know to do
- ○ Your "outer labor" to make your Inspiration become a physical reality

When your Inspiration has been activated and awakened and you have done the inner labor of Introspection to remove the inward blockages in your "pipelines", there is nothing stopping you from Implementing the necessary steps and process to see your life of Inspiration become a reality. Success or fulfillment is not a matter of luck, coincidence, or chance. Living life to your full potential is a guaranteed outcome *if* you consistently utilize the 3 keys in this book. The keys to unlock your dream life, your dream family, and your dream business have now been given to you. So what will you DO with them?

> It is NOW your time for Implementation to experience your life of Inspiration!

Implementation Assignment

Nothing great happens accidentally, coincidentally or by luck. If you want to really live your life of Inspiration, you must be intentional. Success must be scheduled to become a reality. If you don't purposely allocate time to pursue your dreams and goals, then how can you realistically expect it to happen?

The below exercise will focus on utilizing the 3 keys of Inspiration, Introspection, and Implementation. The primary areas we will focus on for this exercise are Family, Career/Business, and Personal. As you openly and honestly answer the questions and Implement the steps below you will be closer than you have ever been to seeing your life of Inspiration become a reality. To not be overwhelming, you should only focus on the #1 change you want to see in each area and focus your thoughts, time, resources, and energy to seeing that change occur. When the results you want begin to show up, then you can duplicate this exercise for additional goals and areas as well. I'm excited for the transformation you will experience!

"Implementation" Game Plan
(Family Goal)

"Unlocked" Questions	"Unlocked" Answers
What is your #1 change or improvement you want to see in your family?	
How will your life be better as a result of this change happening?	
What has held you back from seeing this change up to this point?	
In order to see this change happen, in what ways can "you" change?	
When do you want to see this change occur and what action steps will you take to see it through?	
How can the 3 Keys in this book help this become a reality for you?	

www.pit2palace.org

"Implementation" Game Plan
(Career/Business Goal)

"Unlocked" Questions	"Unlocked" Answers
What is your #1 change or improvement you want to see in your career/business?	
How will your life be better as a result of this change happening?	
What has held you back from seeing this change up to this point?	
In order to see this change happen, in what ways can "you" change?	
When do you want to see this change occur and what action steps will you take to see it through?	
How can the 3 Keys in this book help this become a reality for you?	

"Implementation" Game Plan
(Personal Goal)

"Unlocked" Questions	"Unlocked" Answers
What is your #1 change or improvement you want to see in your personal life?	
How will your life be better as a result of this change happening?	
What has held you back from seeing this change up to this point?	
In order to see this change happen, in what ways can "you" change?	
When do you want to see this change occur and what action steps will you take to see it through?	
How can the 3 Keys in this book help this become a reality for you?	

www.pit2palace.org

Let's "UNLOCK" Your Full Potential!!!

Our Services & Products Include:

- The "Unlocked" Life Online Course
- The "Unlocked" Marriage & Family Seminars
- The "Unlocked" Career & Entrepreneurship Seminars
- The "Unlocked" TRUE YOU Personal Development Seminars
- In-Person & Virtual "Unlocked" Speaking Engagements

$$$ (Ask About Our Referral Payment Program) $$$

We will pay you for anyone you refer who signs up

for any of our products & services.

Visit Our Site To Go Deeper In Your "UNLOCKED" Journey:

www.pit2palace.org

Email Us At:
contact@pit2palace.org

Your True Potential Awaits You!

www.pit2palace.org